SHOPPING

STEWART ROSS

Wayland

Stewart Ross

STARTING HISTORY

Food We Ate
How We Travelled
Our Family
Our Holidays
Our Schools
Shopping
What We Wore
Where We Lived

PICTURE ACKNOWLEDGEMENTS
Chapel Studios 7 (top), 11 (top), 13, 14, 15, 17 (top), 20, 23 (top), 23 (bottom), 24, 27, 29 (top); Paul Crampton 4, 5, 6; B. Gibbs 18; Hulton 11 (bottom), 16, 21, 25, 26; Topham cover 9, 10, 12, 17 (bottom), 19, 22, 28, 30; Wayland Picture Library 8.

Words that appear in **bold** are explained in the glossary on page 31.

Series Editor: Kathryn Smith
Series Designer: Derek Lee

First published in 1992 by
Wayland (Publishers) Ltd
61 Western Road, Hove
East Sussex, BN3 1JD

© Copyright 1992 Wayland (Publishers) Ltd

British Library Cataloguing in Publication Data
Ross, Stewart
Shopping.—(Starting History)
I. title
381.1

ISBN 0 7502 0333 1

Typeset by Dorchester Typesetting Group Ltd
Printed and bound in Belgium by Casterman S.A.

Starting History is designed to be used as source material for Key Stage One of the National History Curriculum. The main text and photographs reflect the requirements of AT1 (Understanding history in its setting) and AT3 (Acquiring and evaluating historical information). The personal accounts are intended to introduce different points of view (AT2 – Understanding points of view and interpretations), and suggestions for activities and further research (AT3 – Development of ability to acquire evidence from historical sources) can be found on page 30.

CONTENTS

IN THE HIGH STREET

This is a picture of the **high street** in a town today. It is full of people doing their shopping, but there are no cars. Is there a high street like this near you?

Shopping has changed a lot over the last eighty years. This street has changed, too. On the next page you will see how.

Here is the same high street during the **Second World War**. It has been bombed. Many shops and houses have been knocked down. People could not go shopping in the high street. After the war new, bigger shops were built in this street.

Look at this picture of the same street. It was taken in 1908. Compare it to the first two photographs. Now you can see all sorts of changes. There are no cars and the street is narrower. The shops are different from modern ones, too.

Molly Evans has been shopping in the same high street for sixty years.

'Changes? My high street has changed completely since I was young. I used to know all the shopkeepers by name. They knew me too. We used to chat for hours. In the 1930s, I used to wander down the high street all morning. I called in at many shops. Now I can find all I want in one store. But I miss the chatting.'

This boy is choosing some apples from a shelf in a **supermarket**. Look how many different kinds there are to choose from! There were no supermarkets when your grandparents were children. People did their shopping in lots of small shops. Where did they buy apples?

These women are at a **sale** in a **department store**. They are shopping for **bargains**. Before supermarkets, department stores were the biggest type of shop. They sold all sorts of different things.

How can you tell that this is not a modern photograph? Look at the woman's clothes. If you look very carefully you can see the prices of the things for sale.

The picture was taken in 1934. At that time there was no **self-service** in shops.

Gilbert Wood remembers working in his small grocery shop.

'This shop belonged to my dad before my wife and me. We knew all our **customers** and always tried to be helpful. But in 1965 a big supermarket opened next door. Its prices were much lower than ours. When our customers started using the supermarket, we had to close our shop.'

This bus is waiting to take people shopping in the middle of town. They have left their cars in a car-park, away from the shops.

Nowadays many town centres do not allow traffic. Cars and lorries are noisy and dirty, and there is not enough room to park.

Here is a village store in 1953. It sold all sorts of things. Which **goods** can you still buy today?

In the past most people walked to the shops because they were near by. Today many people have to go shopping by car or bus.

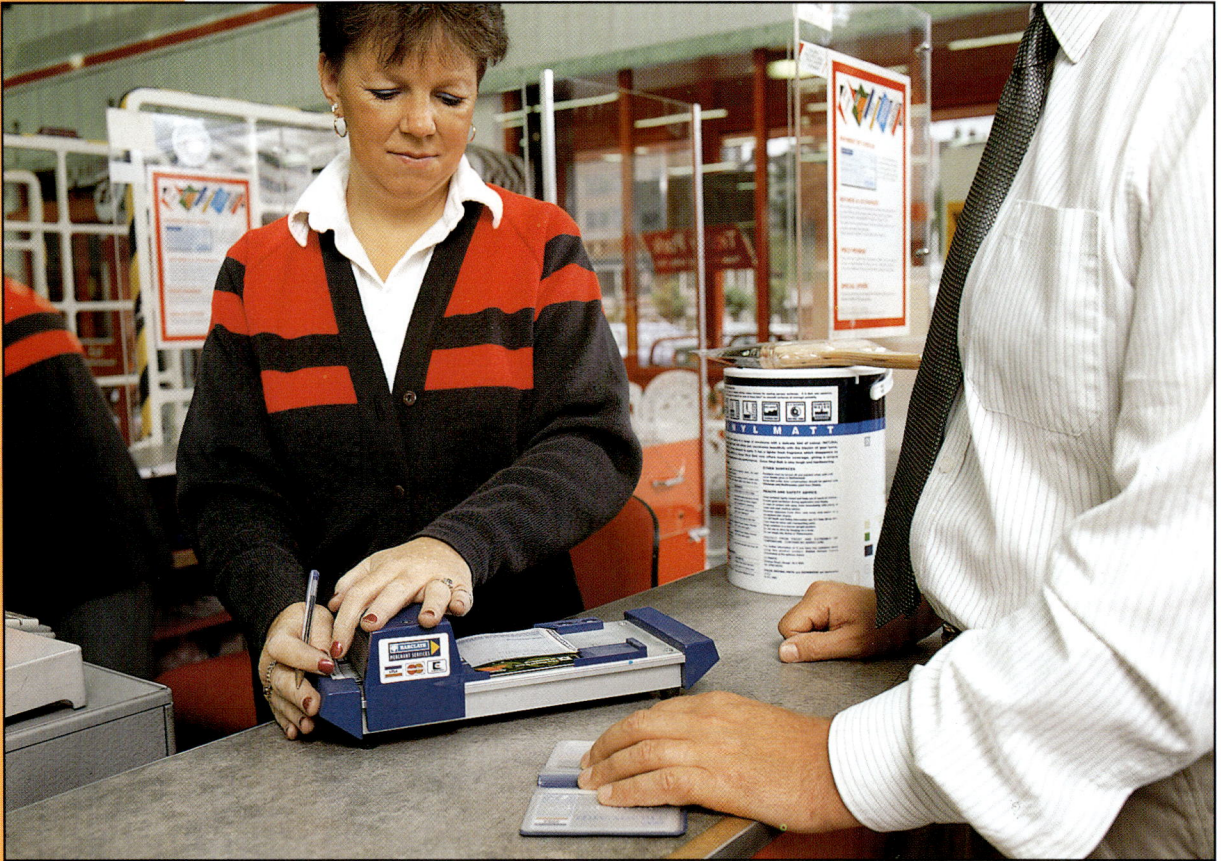

Have you seen anyone paying with a card like this? People can also pay for things with a **cheque** or **cash**.

Cards are a new idea. Thirty years ago most people paid for things with cash. How do your parents pay for the things they buy?

Before 15 February, 1971, people in Britain used a different sort of money. It was called pounds, shillings and pennies. There were twenty shillings in a pound, and twelve pennies in a shilling. Isn't that difficult? No wonder it was changed!

Here is a fish and chip shop in 1953, about forty years ago. Look at the signs on the left of the picture. The prices are shown in the old sort of money. A large bag of fish and chips costs one shilling – that's about 5p today.

In 1971 Margaret Jones had to learn about the new money.

'The supermarket where I worked gave me lessons about the new money. It wasn't very difficult, but some of the older customers took ages to get used to it. They didn't believe there were one hundred pence in a pound. Today no one thinks of old money any more. Who knows what a shilling is?'

17

Customers can fill up their cars with petrol at this modern garage. They can also buy food, drinks and sweets in the shop.

Garages have changed a lot in the last forty years. You can see how by looking at the next picture.

How is this picture of a garage different from the last one? It was taken over forty years ago, after the Second World War.

In those days garages only sold petrol, and there was no self-service. A petrol-pump **assistant** put petrol in the cars.

This is a modern shopping centre. There are lots of shops inside one huge building. Many people like to shop in shopping centres, because there are a lot of shops very close together. If it rains you do not get wet.

This is one of the first ever supermarkets. It was opened in 1955. Today almost everyone buys their **groceries** at a supermarket.

Supermarket shopping is quick and easy. But you cannot chat to the assistants – they are too busy.

You don't see many shops like this one nowadays. It is an **ironmonger's**. What sort of things does it sell?

The woman has her shopping in a paper parcel, tied up with string. Today, most shopkeepers put the things we buy into plastic bags.

I REMEMBER . . .

Jane Fielding does not like shopping in big modern stores.

'The woman in the picture is buying lots of things. But I don't like these big shops. I went to one to buy some green paint. Inside it was huge, like a railway station, with signs everywhere. I couldn't find the paint. I had to ask an assistant to help me. When he said there were six kinds of green paint, I gave up and went home.'

Have you been to a boot fair like this one? People are selling all sorts of things. They have brought everything here in the boots of their cars, or vans.

Thirty years ago there weren't any boot fairs. Not many people had cars.

Is there a market near where you live? You can buy things very cheaply there. In the past many families did all their shopping at the market.

Markets are a very old idea. A long time ago there were no shops, just **stalls** in the street, like this one.

This is a picture of a town on market day in 1940. Animals were often sold in the middle of the street like this. Ask your grandparents if they can remember market day.

Can you see the boy who is looking after the sheep? He looks bored!

This family is shopping at home using a mail order catalogue. The catalogue is full of bright pictures of things to buy. When the family have chosen what they want, they will send their money off. The shopping will arrive in the post.

You could call this van a shop on wheels. Some people live so far from a town that shopkeepers come to their houses. This van is bringing groceries.

You don't often see vans like this nowadays. More people have cars, so they can drive to the shops.

Francis Williams used to sell fruit at markets.

'Here I am selling from the back of my van in 1949. I drove around the country, stopping at all the towns on market day. Big crowds came to listen to me. I told funny stories as I was selling the fruit. There are still lots of markets today, but not like they used to be. Most people go to the supermarket instead.'

Talking to people

Ask some grown-ups what they can remember about shopping in the past. Write down your questions and do an interview, like a TV reporter. How much did things cost? What did they buy and where? If you know someone who lived during the Second World War, ask them how the war changed shopping.

Using your eyes

Old photographs, films and the pictures in books and magazines can tell you a lot about the history of shopping. Old postcards often have pictures of old streets on them, too. There might even be an old-fashioned shop in your town, which has been there since your parents were young. Sometimes the sign at the front of a shop will tell you how old it is.

Shops on display

Why not make a display showing how a street near you has changed since your grandparents were children? It might have been bombed during the Second World War. Which is the oldest shop on the street? Which is the newest shop? You could ask a grown-up if they can remember what some of the shops were like when they were young.

GLOSSARY

Assistants   People who work in shops.

Bargain   Something which is good value.

Cash   Money.

Cheque   A piece of paper you write on to pay for things. It tells the bank to give someone a certain amount of your money.

Customer   A person who buys something at a shop.

Department store   A large shop which sells clothes and things for the house.

Goods   Anything we buy.

Groceries   Food and drink.

High street   The main street in a town.

Ironmonger's   A shop which sells things we need for the house, but not clothes and food.

Sale   When goods are sold at special low prices.

Second World War   The War which lasted from 1939 to 1945. The fighting spread around the world.

Self-service   When people help themselves in a shop, before paying.

Stalls   The tables used to put things on at markets.

Supermarket   A big self-service shop which sells food and drink.

INDEX